A Solicitor's Guide to Moving Home

Andrew Milne

authorHOUSE®

AuthorHouse™ UK Ltd.
500 Avebury Boulevard
Central Milton Keynes, MK9 2BE
www.authorhouse.co.uk
Phone: 08001974150

First published by AuthorHouse 1/27/2010

ISBN: 978-1-4490-4849-5 (sc)

This book is printed on acid-free paper.

In loving Memory of Julie Faultless-
the best Secretary I could have asked for.

Contents

INTRODUCTION

This is my experience of over fifteen years dealing in conveyancing. Some Solicitors may be different to me, but I will explain what a Solicitor needs to do and how you can assist him or her, to make your move more enjoyable and less stressful.

This book is not meant to or is able to replace your Solicitor. It is aimed to specifically guide you along the way and help you understand what your Solicitor needs to do.

Please note that the law is always changing and this book can therefore only be used as a guide, based on the present law. At the end of this book, I have included a glossary of legal terms relating to the conveyancing process, which you may find helpful.

Moving house can be a very stressful time even for the experienced mover, but this is mainly because people are unaware of the procedure, and do not know what their Solicitor is required to do. It is the biggest financial commitment you are likely to make during your lifetime, and it is therefore worthwhile for you to take a while and read and use this book as a helpful guide to the process. Keeping this book close by, and referring to it at different stages of the transaction, will hopefully assist you in understanding what is involved.

In general, a conveyancing transaction takes between eight and twelve weeks to complete. The timescale does however depend on how many parties are in the conveyancing chain, whether parties require a mortgage and how fast each party wishes to move! You will find that the larger the chain, the longer it usually takes, and that a cash buyer can normally proceed quicker than one who requires a mortgage.

Let's get started!

Andrew Milne

CHAPTER 1
THE HOME INFORMATION PACK

It is now a legal requirement for you to obtain a Home Information Pack (a "HIP")

before you market your property for sale.

Therefore, as soon as you have decided to put your house on the market, you will need to instruct a suitably qualified person to prepare a HIP for you. Most Conveyancing Solicitors can provide this service to you and so can Estate Agents, usually through a third party.

The requirement to obtain a HIP applies if you wish to market your property yourself or through an Estate Agent. It is the responsibility of the Seller to compile the HIP and to pay for it!

A HIP contains the following information:-

- an index
- a Sale Statement
- Property Information Questionnaire

- an Energy Performance Certificate ("EPC")
- proof of ownership
- a local authority search
- a water and drainage search
- a copy of the Lease (if your property is leasehold)
- guarantees/warranties/planning consents (where applicable)

HIPs have been introduced to hopefully speed up the selling process by making important information about the Property available at the onset to interested buyers and their Solicitors.

The majority of properties which are sold nowadays require a HIP and for the purposes of this book I will assume that this is the case with your transaction.

So what are the important elements of a HIP? They are as follows:

(1)   Sale Statement

This confirms who is selling the property ("the Seller"), whether it is a flat, or a house and whether the property is freehold or leasehold. When you buy a property in England or Wales, it could be classed as either freehold, leasehold or in rare instances, commonhold.

If the Seller owns a freehold property, this means they own both the building and the land on which the building is situated.

If the property is leasehold, the Seller, known either as a Tenant or a Leaseholder, has the benefit of a Lease granted over the land on which the property is built. I discuss leasehold property in more detail later on in this chapter and in Chapter 4.

(2)   Property Information Questionnaire ("PIQ")

This Questionnaire is completed by the Seller and provides information about the property to help potential buyers decide whether to view or purchase.

It includes questions about flooding and changes which may have been made to the property and which utility services are connected. It has been designed to be quick and easy for the Sellers to complete.

For leasehold properties, the PIQ includes a summary of the leasehold arrangements.

(3)   Energy Performance Certificate ("EPC")

This is a certificate giving information on the energy efficiency of the property, a topic which is very important nowadays. In these times of "global warming" it is hoped that people will want to buy environmentally friendly properties and the EPC is now an integral part of the selling process. It provides a rating for the property as well as listing the potential rating that the property could achieve if you made the recommended changes. Please note that as a Seller, you are under no obligation to carry out any recommendations in the certificate. A fully qualified energy assessor will need to visit your property to compile this report, and therefore needs to be arranged as soon as you have instigated the HIP. Details of the EPC will also be included on the Estate Agents Sales Particulars for the property.

(4)   Proof of ownership

This documentation confirms the identity of the person who owns or is selling the property, and comprises either Land Registry official copy register entries or copies of your unregistered title deeds.

Nowadays the majority of properties in England and Wales are registered at the Land Registry. If so, the Land Registry hold information about the property in electronic format to include who owns it, whether it is freehold or leasehold and details concerning the title to the property.   This information is contained in one document known as "Official Copies". The Land Registry will also hold in their records a plan of the boundaries of the property, which although does not confirm the legal boundaries, can be used for guidance purposes (known as a "filed plan") These records are open to public inspection. Most Solicitors will have internet access to the Land Registry, which can inform you whether or not the property in question is registered.   If the property is registered, Official Copies and the filed plan can be downloaded immediately by the person preparing the HIP.

If your property is not registered at the Land Registry it means that you will have unregistered title deeds, which usually consist of several documents and deeds evidencing that you own your property. The fact that you may have unregistered title deeds does not mean that there is a problem in proving that you own your property, but it does mean that whoever is preparing the HIP needs to be in receipt of these documents before they can complete this section of the HIP. If your property is subject to a mortgage, your Mortgage Lender will be holding these deeds and a request will need to be made (usually through your Solicitor) before these deeds can be released.

Collectively, official copies and unregistered title deeds are known as "the title documents" and are the proof to a Buyer's Solicitors that the Seller has the right to sell the property in question. If you are selling a property on behalf of someone who has died, the HIP will need to include a copy of the Grant of Representation which you will have obtained from the Probate Registry, together with the title documents of the deceased person whose property you are selling.

(5)   Local Authority Search

This Search is set of standardised questions concerning the property relating to information about it held by the Local Authority. Although it is called a "local" search this is slightly misleading, as the majority of the questions on the Search relate only to the property itself and not the local area. The Search will reveal amongst other things, if any recent planning consents have been obtained for the property, whether or not it is in a conservation area, and whether there is any tree preservation order on any trees located on the property. It will confirm if the property is likely to be affected by any nearby traffic schemes, as well as stating whether or not the road on which the property is located is a public or private road. The Local Search usually takes approximately five to ten days to be received.

The Local Search can either be prepared by the Local Authority (called "an official Local Search") or a private company who visit the Local Authority to obtain answers to the necessary questions (called "a personal Local Search").

(6)   Water and drainage search

This search confirms whether or not the property is connected to the public foul and surface water sewers and the water mains. The public foul sewer is the sewer that carries waste water. Some rural properties are not connected to the public foul sewer and instead these properties are served with a septic tank or sewerage treatment system.   The surface water sewer carries the rainwater.   The water mains carry your drinking water.

The search will also confirm if there is a public sewer running through the boundaries of the property, and if so, this means that the local water undertaker will have rights of access to the property if a problem arises concerning the sewer, and it will also mean that you will be restricted as to building any extensions or buildings near to the public sewer, without their consent.

Usually public sewers are located in the road to where the property is located and generally the drains connecting the property to the public sewers are private drains and the maintenance of them is the responsibility of the property owner.

This search takes approximately five days to be received.

(7)   Lease

If the property is leasehold, the HIP must include a copy of the Lease, and I will discuss leasehold properties further in Chapter 4.

Your HIP will usually take between seven to ten days to prepare and will either be in a paper or electronic version, depending on who has prepared it. If your solicitor has prepared the HIP, he will forward it to your Estate Agents, as any prospective buyer is entitled to request to see a copy of the HIP, free of charge.

Hopefully once your HIP has been prepared it won't be too long before a prospective buyer turns into your buyer...

CHAPTER 2
INSTRUCTING YOUR SOLICITOR

Once a sale has been agreed, the next step is to choose a Solicitor, unless as a Seller, you have already appointed one to prepare your HIP.

Many Solicitors nowadays have websites, so if you do have Internet access, log on and have a look to find your local Solicitor. If you do not have access to the Internet, pop down to your local Solicitors' office for a quote and an initial chat. Many people rely on a two-minute telephone quote to decide which Solicitor to use. This method may work for some, but meeting your proposed or existing Solicitor face to face, is going to relax you and make you feel more comfortable from the very earliest stage. Most Solicitors will be only too happy to spare a few minutes to see you and gain that new client or take instructions from an existing client! It also gives you the opportunity to express any concerns or timescales you may have about the transaction.

Once you have decided which Solicitor is to act for you, you need to notify the Estate Agent, if applicable. Alternatively, if you have already met with your Solicitor, he or she will be willing to give the Estate Agent a telephone call themselves, to confirm that they have been instructed by you. The Estate Agent will then type up and send the Confirmation of Sale details (sometimes called the Memorandum of Sale) to the Seller and Buyer and their respective Solicitors. This confirms the details of the parties and their solicitors and the the agreed sale price. This Confirmation of Sale is very useful for the Solicitors in that it enables us to contact the other Solicitor to get the ball rolling!

Once the Confirmation of Sale has been received by the respective solicitors, they will be contacting their client if this has not already been done, to confirm instructions. Your Solicitor is likely to deal with the following points at this stage:-

1. For money laundering purposes, you will be required to provide some form of identification, which would normally be your passport or photo drivers licence, as well as confirmation of your present address, by way of a recent utility bill.
2. If you are the Buyer search fees will be requested. Your Solicitor will need to carry out searches on your behalf, all of which are mentioned in Chapter 4.
3. You will receive details of your likely legal costs, as well as a breakdown of the disbursements (out of pocket expenses which your Solicitor will incur on your behalf during the transaction).
4. You will receive a Terms of Engagement/Client Care Letter which sets out the conditions on which your Solicitor will act for you.
5. If you are selling, your Solicitor will ask you for your Mortgage account number (if you have a mortgage

over the property) and ask you to complete a Property Information Form and a Fittings and Contents Form.

At this stage it is useful to give you some handy tips as follows:-

(a)   Please remember that your Solicitor cannot talk directly to the other party in the transaction, but has to correspond with their Solicitor. Your Estate Agent can however contact the other party directly, and if you have any questions which you feel your Solicitor does not need to get involved with, please deal with these through the Estate Agents. Alternatively, if you and the other party are happy to have close contact with one another, exchange telephone numbers, so you can keep in touch throughout the transaction.

(b)   If you are a buyer, and you need to arrange a mortgage, feel free to speak to your Solicitor who should be able to recommend an independent financial adviser to assist you in this process.

(c)   If you are a buyer, it is useful at this stage for you to notify your Solicitor of any extensions to the property so that he knows well in advance to check that the appropriate planning consents have been obtained.

CHAPTER 3
The Contract Package

Once the Seller's Solicitor has received the Confirmation of Sale from the Estate Agents, it is necessary for him to prepare a Contract pack which is forwarded to the Buyer's Solicitors. This pack will include the Contract, the Property Information Forms and Fittings and Contents Forms and a copy of the HIP. If an Estate Agent has prepared the HIP, they will usually have sent a copy or a link for the HIP to both the Seller's and the Buyer's Solicitors at the time of sending out the Confirmation of Sale.

The Contract confirms the identities of the parties to the transaction, whether the property to be sold is freehold or leasehold, the sale price, and the conditions of sale. The Seller's Solicitor prepares the Contract by referring to the title documents in the HIP. One copy of the Contract is retained by the Seller's Solicitor and the other copy is sent to the Buyer's Solicitor, so that in due course, both the Seller and the Buyer can sign their respective copy.

The Property Information Form and the Fittings and Contents Forms now need to be completed by the Seller. All the information on these forms can be relied on by the Buyer and it is therefore important that the information provided is correct and accurate.

On the Fittings and Contents Forms, the Seller need to indicate what items in the Property are to be included in the sale price and what items are to be excluded. The list includes carpets, curtains and light fittings amongst many others and you will be under a legal obligation to leave the items that you have said are included in the sale price, on completion of the sale.

If there are any items (eg washing machine or cooker) that you have not agreed are included in the sale price, but are willing to sell to the Buyer for an additional sum, you can stipulate this on the form.

The Property Information Form asks an array of questions about the property and although the majority of them are straightforward, please take your time to answer them and ask your Solicitor if you have any doubts about any of them.

Probably one of the most important questions asked is whether or not any building works have been carried out to the property. These building works may comprise of extensions or the construction of a conservatory, or the conversion of a garage to a playroom/office. As more and more properties nowadays are being extended or converted, the question as to whether or not the appropriate planning consents have been obtained for these works is a common one. As far as the Seller's and Buyer's Solicitors are concerned, making sure that the correct planning consents have been obtained for the property their client is either selling or buying, is crucial.

Planning consents can comprise either of Building Regulations Approval or Planning Permission. Whenever structural alterations are made to a property, Building Regulations Approval is normally required. This approval is obtained from the Local Authority, and nowadays the Local Authority Building Inspector will visit the property at key stages of the work to make sure that it is being carried out in accordance with current Building Regulations standards. Once all the work has been completed, the Building Inspector will issue a completion certificate if he is satisfied that the work has been carried out in compliance with Building Regulations. Accordingly, if there has been a recent extensions carried out to the property which required Building Regulations Approval, then the Buyer's Solicitor needs to make sure that a completion certificate has been issued.

If recent structural alterations have been carried out to the property and the completion certificate cannot be produced, this may cause problems for the Buyer's Solicitor, as he is under a duty to his client, as well as the Mortgage lender (if the Buyer is having a Mortgage) that all planning consents have been obtained. If the completion certificate cannot be produced, the Buyer's Solicitor cannot verify that the work had been carried out to Building Regulations standards. If this is the case, it is usual for the Seller to agree to pay for Building Regulations Indemnity Insurance. This is a one-off modest payment made to an insurance company and which insurance protects the Buyer if, at a later date, the Local Authority takes enforcement action because the work does not comply with the Building Regulations standards. However, this insurance does not protect the Buyer from any faulty workmanship or any cost in putting right a badly made extension! It is therefore most advisable for any Buyer to have their own surveyor check any extensions carried out to a property he may be purchasing, if a completion certificate has not been produced.

As well as Building Regulations Approval, Planning Permission may also have been required depending on the size of the extension or the Local Authority's policy. If required, this permission needs to be obtained before any building works are commenced. The recent Planning Permission history for a property will be revealed in the Buyer's Local Authority Search (see Chapter 1), and again it is important for the Seller to notify his Solicitor if Planning Permission has been obtained for any extension to the property, so that if the Seller has not retained a copy, his Solicitor can obtain one, at a fee, from the Local Authority. The Planning Permission can then be forwarded to the Buyer's Solicitor with the Contract package, and will satisfy his enquiries concerning the same. If Planning Permission has not been obtained for a large extension, the Buyer's Solicitor will need to be happy that such Planning Permission was not required, as Local Authorities do have the power to request that extensions be pulled down in circumstances where Planning Permission was not obtained, when it should have been!

Please note that if you are purchasing a property which is in a conservation area or is a graded or listed building, other consents need to be obtained from the Local Authority before any alterations or extensions are carried out and you should therefore obtain specialist advice from your Solicitor in these circumstances.

If not included in the HIP, the Contract pack will also include any other documents which may be relevant to the property, and these may include the following:-

- Any guarantees relating to the property (e.g. double glazing/roofing guarantees);
- If the property is less than ten years old, it may have Builder's ten year guarantee (e.g. NHBC/Zurich cover);
- Any central heating service contract and
- Timber/damp guarantees

As well as forwarding the contract pack to the Buyer's Solicitors, at this stage the Seller's Solicitors will normally request a mortgage redemption statement from the Seller's mortgage lender, if applicable. This statement confirms how much money is presently outstanding under the Seller's mortgage, and it will also provide confirmation as to whether or not there is an early redemption charge if the mortgage is paid off within any time period. It is good practice for the Seller's Solicitor to forward a copy of this redemption statement to his client once it has been received, so that you are aware of this information at an early stage in the transaction.

Upon receipt of the Contract pack, the Buyer's Solicitor now needs to check that everything is in order ...

CHAPTER 4

Investigating the Title

Upon receipt of the Contract pack and the HIP from the Seller's Solicitor, the Buyer's Solicitor will need to do several things which can be broken down as follows:-

(i)   Check the HIP
(ii)   Check the Title Documents for the property;
(iii)   Report to the Buyer concerning the Property Information Form and the Fittings and Contents Form;
(iv)   Put in hand Searches;
(v)   Read the Lease (if the property is leasehold); and
(vi)   Raise any necessary enquiries with the Seller's Solicitor.

(i)   Checking the HIP

The Buyer's Solicitor will go through the contents of the HIP and will send a copy to the Buyer if he wishes one. As far as the Buyer's Solicitor is concerned the most important aspects of the HIP are the title documents and the Searches it contains, and I discuss these later on in this chapter.

(ii)   Checking the Title documents to the property

As mentioned in Chapter 1, the HIP will contain a copy of the title documents to the property. The Buyer's Solicitor will check to make sure that the Sellers are shown on the title as owning the property, or if not, that they have the power to sell the property. He will also check to see whether the property is freehold or leasehold and whether any covenants or easements affect the property. There may be covenants stating that the property shall only be used as a private dwellinghouse or that the consent of the original landowner or builder is required before any extensions to the property are carried out. Fencing covenants are also common, and these confirm which boundary fences the owner of the property is responsible for maintaining. It is not always the right hand fence!

As regards easements, the Title documents may state if there is any common right of way over the property or whether an adjoining landowner has the right of access to the property for the purpose of maintaining any common sewer, for example. All these issues are most important and need to be studied by the Buyer's Solicitor in great detail to make sure that everything is in order.

If the property is leasehold, time will be taken to read through the Lease.

(iii)   Report to the Buyer's on Property Information Form and Fittings and Contents Form

The Buyer's Solicitor will need to send his client a copy of the Property Information Form and Fittings and Contents

Form and it is good practice to also forward a copy plan of the property. It is most important that the Buyer reads and checks the forms, to make sure that the information in them meets with their understanding. In particular, you may have agreed with the Seller that certain fittings and contents are to be included in the sale price, and it is therefore important to check that these items are included on the Fittings and Contents Form as being included. The Property Information Form gives the Buyer general information concerning the property but there is also a section asking the Seller to confirm whether or not he has any suggested completion date in mind, and if this date varies from the Buyer's understanding, it is best to raise this point at this stage. The Buyer should also take time to check that any plan forwarded appears to be accurate, because you will only be receiving legal ownership of the land referred to in the Title documents. If a piece of land appears to be missing from the plan, please raise this with your Solicitor, who can raise an enquiry with the Seller's Solicitor.

If you are buying a property other than to use it as a private dwellinghouse, it might be advisable to let your Solicitor know at this stage so that he can check the Title documents to make sure that there is no covenant preventing you from using the property for your intended purpose.

(iv)   Put in hand Searches

There are certain desk-top Searches which must be carried out by the Buyer's Solicitor, if his client is having a Mortgage, and which will be recommended to you even if you are a cash Buyer. Please note that if the property has a HIP, two of these searches, the local authority search and the water/

drainage searches, which I have discussed in Chapter 1, will be included and hence it will not normally be necessary for the Buyer's Solicitors also to carry out these searches unless they are approaching six months in age. If you are having a mortgage it will be a requirement that all searches are less than six months old at the date of completion, and in these circumstances, you, as the buyer, will have to pay for these searches, as the seller is not under a duty to update the searches within the HIP!

The other searches which may need to be put in hand are as follows:

(a)   Environmental Search
        The Environmental Search looks at the past use of the land using historical data, to see if there is potentially any contamination on the property. Under recent changes in legislation, an owner of a property may be responsible for clearing up any contamination which is present on his land, and Solicitors are therefore advised to carry out this search on behalf of clients. The search also reveals whether or not there are any landfill sites in close proximity to the property, as well as confirming other environmental issues. This search takes between 1 to 3 days to receive.

(b)   Chancel Search
        Most Solicitors will carry out this search, which confirms whether or not there is a possibility that the property you are purchasing may be liable to contribute to repairs to the chancel part of the local Church of England or Wales Church. Although this law stems back many years it is still appropriate today. Unfortunately, at present, there is no central record to confirm which properties in England and Wales are

affected. However, it is hoped that a central record will be available in or around 2012. If the search reveals that there is a liability or potential liability, your Solicitor will be able to advise you on this and suitable insurance can be taken out to protect you in the event of you ever receiving a request for payment from the Church!

There are also several further searches which may need to be carried out by your Solicitor depending on which area of the country the property is situated. For example a Coal Mining Report is required in areas of previous and present coal mining, such as parts of the Midlands. Your Solicitor should be aware of which additional searches are required. There are also further optional searches which your Solicitor can carry out for you, namely a Know Your Neighbour Search and a Planning Search. The Know Your Neighbour Search gives you information and statistics concerning the area in which the property is situated, and the Planning Search confirms what planning applications have been made within the locality of the property. Both these Searches are relatively cheap, and do provide very useful additional information to Buyer.

All Searches nowadays can be done over the internet, if your Solicitor has the system in place. If not, they are carried out through the post although this does usually prolong the time in which the results are received, by a couple of days or so. Once any of the Searches are received by your Solicitor he will forward a copy to you if the results reveal any issues which he thinks you need to be made aware of.

Remember your Solicitor will not usually put in hand these Searches until you have provided him with sufficient funds. So the quicker you do this, the quicker the searches can be obtained. Some Buyers however prefer to wait to make sure that the result of their survey is satisfactory, or that their Mortgage has been approved, before instructing their Solicitor to carry out the Searches.

(v)   Leasehold Properties

The Contract and the HIP will confirm whether or not the Property you are purchasing is freehold or leasehold. As mentioned in Chapter 1, a leasehold property which can be a house or a flat, is one where the land itself is owned by a third party, known as the Landlord, who has granted a Lease to the occupier (known as the Tenant or the Leaseholder).

A Lease is an agreement allowing the Tenant to remain on the Landlord's land and have use of the building on it, for a certain length of time. Typically Leases are granted for a period of 99 or 125 years, but can be of any length!

A copy of the Lease will be included within the HIP, and the Buyer's Solicitors will need to study it to make sure that the terms of it are satisfactory. He will first check to see how many years are remaining on the Lease. Although all Banks/ Building Societies have difference criteria, generally there must be at least 55 years remaining on the term of the lease for a Bank/Building Society to grant a mortgage over it. The Mortgage Lender will not have checked this information at the time of your mortgage application, so the onus is on the Buyer's Solicitor to check that this condition is met.

The Lease will normally contain the following important information:

- what yearly rent is payable to the Landlord by the Tenant (known as "ground rent");
- whether it is the responsibility of the Landlord or the Tenant to arrange the Buildings Insurance;
- whether the Landlord's consent is required for any alterations to the property;
- what covenants affect the property which the Buyer's will need to comply with and
- in the case of a flat or maisonette, who is responsible for maintaining the structure and communal parts of the building. Usually this cost will be paid by the Tenant under what is called a "Service Charge".

As well as receiving a copy of the Lease, the Buyer's Solicitors will also obtain from the Seller's Solicitor details of the payment of Ground Rent and Service Charge and ensure that they are paid up-to-date and will want to see any yearly accounts which may have been prepared by the Landlord in respect of the Service Charge.

The Seller will also have completed a Leasehold Information Form which asks various questions about the Lease and a copy of this will normally be forwarded to the Buyer.

The above is only a brief outline guide to leasehold properties and as the wording of leases are all slightly different, your Solicitor will be on hand to advise you, as these transactions are a little more involved.

(vi)   Raising enquiries with the Seller's Solicitor

Having checked all the above documentation and having spoken to his client about any possible queries, the Buyer's Solicitor will raise any additional enquiries concerning the property with the Seller's Solicitor. Again, if you do have specific questions concerning the property, get your Solicitor to raise them at this stage.

CHAPTER 5
Survey or Valuation Report?

While the Solicitors are dealing with the Contract and the Buyer's Solicitor is putting in hand the searches, it is up to the Buyer to make arrangements concerning his Mortgage, if he is having one, as well as arranging a survey.

Survey

If the Buyer is having a Mortgage, the Buyer will have the choice of either having a Valuation Report carried out, or a full survey, (often known as a HomeBuyer's Report.) As a Buyer, you buy the property in its existing condition, subject to any defects there may be. Therefore, once you have moved into the property it is your responsibility if any repairs are required. It is therefore advisable to find out if any such repairs will be necessary, so that you are aware of the position, and if these are major repairs, quotes can be obtained and you will then have a bargaining tool to go back to the Seller as regards a price reduction.

I would say that most Buyers normally rely on the Valuation Report carried out by their Mortgage lender. This report is carried out by a surveyor but is not a survey as such, and is carried out for the benefit of the Mortgage lender, to check that the property is adequate security for the amount of money they will be lending you. The Valuation Report usually takes the surveyor approximately 20 to 30 minutes to conduct, and it will entail him having a quick look around the property to make sure the property is in a good state of repair, and that the purchase price does not reflect an under-valuation or over-valuation of the property. If the surveyor feels that the Buyer is paying more for the property than his valuation of it, this may affect the amount of Mortgage the Buyer can obtain.

As mentioned, it may be wiser to have a full survey carried out, bearing in mind that buying a house is likely to be your biggest financial commitment. For the sake of a few hundred pounds, it is better to know what in fact you are purchasing in order to give you peace of mind. Would you, for example, buy a car from a stranger without having it fully checked over?

Whether you are having a mortgage or not you can instruct a local Chartered Surveyor to carry out a full survey for you. Your Solicitor will be able to recommend a local Surveyor for you. The usual survey is called a Home Buyer's Report and is much more detailed than a basic valuation report. The Surveyor will give an estimate of what he believes is the current market value of the property and what repairs may be needed.

The Survey will give you a good overview of the general state and condition of the property, and will cover all visible parts of the main building and any other permanent outbuildings the property may have. The Surveyor will also inspect those parts of the electricity, gas/oil, water, heating and drainage services that can be seen, although he will not test them. Any necessary repairs or defects are set out in the Survey, detailing whether these are serious or routine.

For Buildings Insurance purposes, the Report will also confirm the amount the property should be insured for. This figure is calculated on how much it would cost to rebuild the property in the event that it had been destroyed and is known as the reinstatement value. This figure is not therefore the same as the purchase price!

If the property you are buying is older in age, or of an unusual construction, you may consider having a Building Survey as opposed to a Home Buyer's Report. This type of Survey also provides a full picture of the property's construction and condition and it goes into more detail than the Home Buyer's Report, so is more expensive. You will be able to discuss your needs with the Surveyor and he will be able to advise you as to which survey is best for you.

Whether you have a Valuation or a Survey, either of them may recommend further reports which are necessary. For example, if any damp has been detected, a timber and damp report will be recommended, or if there appears to be any structural problems, then a structural report will be needed. Of course it is vital that you have these further reports carried out, to check whether or not there is a problem, and if work is required, the likely cost of it. As mentioned, if any repairs are required, it is perfectly acceptable for you to go back to the Seller and ask for a price reduction, or at least a contribution towards the cost of carrying out these repairs. If you are having a Mortgage, and the repairs are serious, your Mortgage lender will normally request a copy of this report, so that their Valuer can assess the situation, and if they feel that this work needs to be carried out as a matter of urgency, they will often stipulate in your Mortgage offer that they will hold back a sum of money from the Mortgage monies until the work has been carried out. This is known as a retention, and can cause problems to the Buyer in that they need the full Mortgage monies to complete the purchase, but the Mortgage lender will not provide the full amount, until the necessary work has been completed. In these circumstances, the ideal position for the Buyer is to get the Seller to carry out these works before completion, although from the Seller's point of view, he may be unwilling to agree to this, unless Contracts have been exchanged. This is because he runs the risk of spending money in getting these repairs done, but has no commitment from the Buyer to proceed with the purchase. Usually, therefore, where a retention is involved, the work will be carried out between exchange of Contracts and completion. Who pays for these works depends entirely on the bargaining power of the Seller and the Buyer in the transaction.

Alternatively, the Buyer can get the work carried out after completion, once he has moved into the property, but only when the work has been completed will the Mortgage lender release the balance of the Mortgage advance. Of course, if major structural problems have been revealed this might mean that the Buyer decides not to proceed with his purchase, if this work is going to be expensive, and a suitable compromise cannot be a reached between the parties.

Top Tips

(i) It is always advisable to have a full survey, even if the property you are purchasing is only a few years old, as problems can arise in properties of any age!

(ii) If you are relying on a Valuation Report carried out by a Mortgage lender, please be aware that some Mortgage lenders do not even insist that their Valuer inspects the property, and they rely on him to drive to the property to check that it appears to be in good repair, from the outside.

(iii) Again, with the Valuation Report, some Mortgage lenders do not provide a copy of the report to the Buyer, and you are therefore in the dark as to what the report says and whether or not there are any defects in the property, although of course if there were major defects, the Mortgage lender is likely to inform you of them, as this might affect whether or not they in fact grant a Mortgage to you. Therefore, please remember to ask your Mortgage lender whether or not you will in fact be receiving a copy of the Valuation Report.

(iv) Remember if works are recommended, please obtain further reports and always ask the Seller to contribute to the cost of any such works, unless of course you were aware of these when you made your offer to purchase the property.

CHAPTER 6
The Mortgage

The majority of Buyers will require a Mortgage to finance their purchase. As it is likely to be your largest monthly outgoing, it is important that you pick the Mortgage best suited to your individual circumstances. So where should you go for advice on your Mortgage?

Many Buyers will have close links with their own Bank, and may feel comfortable speaking to their Bank manager concerning a Mortgage on the basis that the Bank is aware of their financial background.

It is however usually best to obtain advice from an independent financial adviser ("IFA") and your Solicitor or the Estate Agent may be able to recommend one for you. An IFA has no ties with any particular Bank or Building Society and can therefore recommend and allow you to select any of the best mortgage products which are on the market. Furthermore, IFAs often have access to certain Mortgage products which are not otherwise available on the high street.

If you have decided to use an IFA, he will usually make the effort to come and chat to you in the comfort of your own home, providing a free initial consultation without obligation. Some IFAs will not charge a separate fee to you for their services, as they will receive a payment, known as commission, from the Mortgage lender, the details of which you are entitled to be informed about.

First of all, you will need to decide how much you can borrow, although hopefully you will already have established that you can of course afford the property you are purchasing! The amount you can borrow from a Mortgage provider depends on several factors, and all Banks and Building Societies have different criteria. Some Mortgage lenders will, subject to your financial status, grant you a loan of up to 80% to 90% of the value of the property you are purchasing depending on the current market conditions. Once you have decided how much you can borrow, you will need to find out if you can actually afford the repayments, depending on which type of Mortgage you would like.

Although all Mortgages are different, you have one of two choices when it comes to the repayment method of your Mortgage. You can either choose a capital/repayment Mortgage or an interest-only Mortgage.

1.   Capital/repayment Mortgages

Your monthly repayment on this type of Mortgage covers an element of both the interest you owe to the Mortgage lender as well as the element of the capital ("the lump sum") you have borrowed. This means therefore that provided you maintain the monthly payments for the duration of your Mortgage, you are guaranteed to repay the loan at the end of the term.

2.   Interest-only Mortgages

With this type of Mortgage, you pay back only interest to the Mortgage lender. This means that provided you keep up with your Mortgage payments for the duration of the Mortgage, you will still owe to the lender at the end of the term, the capital amount which you borrowed at the start of the Mortgage. The idea of this type of Mortgage is that you have some other investment available at the end of the Mortgage period, which is used to pay back the capital sum to your Mortgage lender. Usually this other investment would be an endowment policy or a pension, separate monthly payments for which you would of course be obliged to pay to enable such an investment to be of an equivalent value to your Mortgage loan, at the end of your Mortgage term. Again your IFA will be able to advise you on any such products.

Once you have chosen the type of repayment method you require, you will also need to decide whether you pick a Mortgage which has a fixed or discounted rate of interest. Again, it all comes down to your individual choice and which the IFA will be able to guide you on.

Once you have agreed on the Mortgage product and which Bank or Building Society you are to apply to, you will need to complete an appropriate application form as well as normally providing a cheque payable to the Mortgage lender for any application fee which may be payable, as well as for any valuation fee. Once the Mortgage lender has received your completed application form, the lender will check your financial status, (often asking for wage slips if you are employed, or accounts if you are self employed), as well as carrying out a credit check against you.

Once the financial checks have been approved, the lender will then instruct their Valuer to do the valuation or HomeBuyer's Report, depending on which report you have opted to have carried out, as mentioned in the previous chapter. Once the surveyor has completed his inspection, his report will be sent to the Mortgage lender for their approval. Provided it is approved, the lender will then issue the Mortgage Offer to you. The Mortgage Offer will set out the terms of your Mortgage and any special conditions which need to be dealt with (for example, if the valuation report has suggested that there may be repairs required to the property, the Mortgage Offer may state that a report on this item of disrepair be carried out, and any recommended works be completed before the Mortgage can be entered into). A copy of your Mortgage Offer is also sent to your Solicitor at the same time as you receive your copy, as usually your Solicitor will also be acting for your Mortgage lender, ensuring that all the legal formalities concerning the Mortgage are dealt with.

Coupled with your Mortgage, you will also need to consider buildings and contents insurance, and life insurance.

It is essential that buildings and contents insurance is arranged, and your Mortgage lender will be able to provide this although you may find that you can get a cheaper deal if you arrange it yourself, or through your IFA. If you do arrange your own buildings and contents insurance, please note that a copy of the policy will be required by your Solicitor, so that he knows that such insurance has been arranged correctly.

Life insurance will also be recommended to you, especially if you are purchasing the property with your spouse or partner. This insurance will cover you in the unfortunate event of you dying during the Mortgage term, and any such insurance is usually for the same sum as your Mortgage amount.

Once you have arranged all of the above, it will now be time to discuss matters with your Solicitor.....

CHAPTER 7
Signing and Exchanging Contracts

If you are the Buyer, once you have received your Mortgage offer, if applicable, and your Solicitor has completed his Searches and enquiries, he will call you into his office for the purpose of discussing and hopefully signing the Contract and other documentation. At this stage, the Buyer's Solicitor will notify the Seller's Solicitor that this is being done, and the Seller will also be invited into his Solicitor's office for the purpose of signing his copy of the Contract also.

As a purchaser, the following points will normally be dealt with at the interview:-

1.   Discussion of the Contract pack
      Your Solicitor will discuss all relevant matters concerning the property which have been revealed in the Contract pack, and which has been supplied by the Seller's Solicitor.
2.   Discuss the Searches, and if applicable, your mortgage offer.

3. <u>Discuss exchange of Contracts</u>.

Your Solicitor will explain that once all parties have signed the Contract, and a date for moving (completion day) has been agreed, the respective parties' Solicitors will exchange Contracts over the telephone. This is when you are legally bound to complete the transaction, and when a completion date is confirmed. **Just by signing the Contract in the Solicitor's office does not commit you to proceed there and then with the transaction. It just means that the Solicitor will be ready to exchange Contracts, on your say-so, once the other parties in the chain are also ready.**

If you are the Buyer, you are under a duty to pay 10% of the purchase price, by way of a deposit, on exchange of Contracts. However, in reality, this does not always happen if your money is tied up in your existing property and what usually happens is that the deposit amount you receive on your sale will be used as a deposit on your purchase.

If you are a first time Buyer, it is usual for your Solicitor to ask you for a sum representing 10% of the purchase price, at this stage, which will then be forwarded to the Buyer's Solicitors once Contracts have been exchanged. However, if you are having more than a 90% mortgage, you will not be able to provide a 10% deposit, and usually the Seller will accept a lesser deposit in these circumstances.

4. **Discussing Completion.**

Most importantly, you will wish to discuss a moving day ("completion") with your Solicitor. It may be that the

Solicitors or parties have already discussed moving dates before the interview, but if not, your Solicitor will ask if you have any specific dates in mind. It is always advisable to discuss completion dates with your Solicitor before agreeing any directly with the other party, so that your Solicitor can inform you if these dates are achievable from his point of view, taking into account any outstanding legal issues.

Usually, completion takes place between seven and fourteen days after Contracts have been exchanged, to enable the Solicitors to finalise matters. Historically, completion usually takes place on a Friday, which gives all parties the weekend to move into the property. Unfortunately completion cannot take place on a Saturday or Sunday, as the majority of Solicitors offices and the Banks are not open on these days! Your Solicitor will explain that on the completion day, once the money has been transferred to the Seller's Solicitor's Bank, that that is when completion has taken place, and that is when the Seller is under a duty to hand over the keys to the Buyer. Unless the property which is being purchased is occupied by a tenant who is to remain in occupation following completion, the Seller is under a duty to give vacant possession at this time, and it is therefore imperative that if you agree a completion date, you are confident that you can get removals for that day and give up vacant possession or otherwise you would be in breach of Contract.

5.   Balance monies

If you are a Buyer, and there are any balances monies required over and above the deposit you are to pay, your Solicitor will advise you as to the amount he requires, and this figure is likely to include the Solicitor's charges as well as the other disbursements, such as Stamp Duty and the Land Registry fee. Your Solicitor will ask for these monies, so that he has cleared funds in time for completion. Therefore, if you are paying by way of a cheque, your Solicitor will normally ask for this at least five working days before completion. Alternatively, if there is a short time period between exchange of Contracts and completion, your Solicitor will ask for either a Banker's draft or a Bank transfer into his firm's client account.

6.   Land Registry Transfer document

If you are the Buyer, you will normally sign the Transfer which is a Land Registry document and which needs to be submitted after completion, to enable the Land Registry to register you as the new owner of the property. If you are purchasing the property in joint names, your Solicitor will advise you of the options you have as to how you would like to own the property with the other party.   If you are a husband and wife, it is usual for you to hold the property as joint tenants. This means that in the unfortunate event of either of you dying, the property would pass automatically through survivorship, to the surviving spouse.

The other option is for you to hold the property as tenants in common. This means that each party owns a separate percentage share in the property, which is the percentage each party is entitled to receive on any eventual sale, or, if either party dies their respective percentage will form part of their estate. You may decide this second option if for example you are in a second marriage, and you wish to leave your share of the property to any children you may have from your first marriage. Unmarried couples may also want to select this option if one party has contributed more of their own savings to the purchase than the other party. There are also other scenarios where the second option may be more favorable, depending on your individual circumstances, and which can be discussed with your Solicitor.

7.   Stamp Duty Land Transaction Form

The Stamp Duty Land transaction form is a form which your Solicitor will normally complete on your behalf, with your authority. Even if Stamp Duty is not payable this form usually still needs to be completed, and it contains details of the purchase transaction to include the price and the parties full names. The form is submitted to HM Revenue and Customs following completion, by the Buyer's Solicitor, together with any payment of Stamp Duty Land Tax if it is payable.

8.   Insurances

In respect of Buildings Insurance, if you are the Seller, your Solicitor will advise you to keep this in place until completion, and if you are a Buyer, it is usual practice for your Buildings Insurance to be put on risk from the date Contracts are exchanged.

If you are having a Mortgage and life cover has been arranged, it is advisable that this insurance is also put in force from the date Contracts are exchanged.

9.   Discussing Wills

Your Solicitor will discuss the importance of making a Will, whether you are a Seller or a Buyer. Most people do not make a Will until much later in their lives, if at all, but as there are strict rules as to who inherits your estate if you die without making a Will, it is most important that everybody makes a Will!

10.   Any questions you have

Your Solicitor will of course ask if you have any other questions which need discussing, and this may include a question as regards what happens with keys on completion. This is discussed in Chapter 8.

11.   Matters for the Seller

If you are selling, your Solicitor will ask for confirmation that the answers given by you on the Property Information Form remains the same, as the Seller is under a duty to notify the Buyer, through his Solicitors, of any matters relating to the property, which have come to light since the date the Property Information Form was completed. For example, the Seller may have received a letter from the Local Authority stating that a next door neighbour has put in a planning application, and this information would have to be disclosed to the Buyer's Solicitor.

Your Solicitor will explain that you will need to give vacant possession of the property on completion, and that therefore all items, other than those items on the Fittings and Contents

Form which you have said are included in the sale, will need to be removed from the property. It also means that any rubbish or contents in the loft, for example, will need to be moved out!

Once all matters have been discussed, and you are happy to proceed, your Solicitor will ask you to sign the Contract!

Once all parties in the transaction have signed their copy of the Contract, the Buyer's deposit has been cleared in his Solicitors' bank account and a completion date has been agreed, the respective Solicitors will be able to exchange Contracts. The actual procedure for exchanging Contracts is relatively straightforward. The respective Solicitors will speak on the telephone and will confirm the terms of the Contract with each other to include confirming the parties names, the sale price, the amount of deposit to be paid by the Buyer and the completion date. The Contract is then dated and the time is noted. Finally, the respective Solicitors agree to post their clients' part of the Contract to the other Solicitor that day, and the Buyer's Solicitor will also send the deposit cheque.

Contracts are now exchanged and your Solicitor will be on the telephone to you to confirm this!

CHAPTER 8

Getting Ready To Move

There is normally a period of seven to fourteen days between exchange of Contracts and completion, and during this time, there is plenty for both Solicitor and client to be dealing with.

Whether you are a Seller or a Buyer, the most important thing you should be doing at this stage is, now that a completion date is known, is confirming and finalising details with your removals Company. As completion usually takes place on a Friday, this is the busiest day of the week for removal Companies as well, so it is time now to make sure your removal Company has confirmation from you of your moving date.

If you have not already done so, you should also be confirming the arrangements as regards picking up or handing over the keys on the completion day. If you have had quite a lot of direct correspondence with the other party, it may be that you agree to hand over the keys directly with them. If not, it is usual for the keys to be delivered to the Seller's Estate

Agents on the morning of completion, once the property in question has been emptied.

Other matters both the Seller and Buyer should be doing at this stage are:-

- Arranging the redirection of post
- Arranging change of address notes for family and friends.

As a Buyer, you should also be checking that your buildings insurance is put in force, although this will automatically be done if you are taking out buildings insurance through your Mortgage Lender. The Solicitors at this stage are also making sure that all legal matters have been finalised.

The Seller's Solicitor will be obtaining a final mortgage statement from the Seller's Bank or Building Society as he will be under a duty to pay off this amount from the proceeds of sale. He will also be receiving the Transfer document from the Buyer's Solicitors and will need to make arrangements for the Seller to call into the office for the purpose of signing it, or alternatively posting it to the Seller, if there is sufficient time. He will also be requesting the Estate Agent's bill, and obtaining his client's approval to it, as this will be paid by the Solicitor on completion, on behalf of the Seller. The Buyer's Solicitor will also be sending the Seller's Solicitor a completion questionnaire (called "Requisitions on Title") which, amongst other things, asks what arrangements will be made concerning the collection of keys as well as requesting confirmation that the answers given by the Seller on the Property Information Form remains unaltered. The Seller's Solicitor will also be giving the Buyer's Solicitor his firm's

Bank details, so that the Buyer's Solicitor knows where to send the balance purchase monies on completion, which is done by way of an electronic Bank transfer.

The Buyer's Solicitor will be requesting his client's mortgage funds at this stage, if applicable, and most Banks and Building Societies require approximately five days notice before releasing these funds. It is good practice for the Buyer's Solicitor to request these funds for the day before completion, which minimises any possible delay on completion. If this is done, the client should be notified that most Mortgage Lenders charge interest on the mortgage amount from the date the funds are released to their Solicitor.

The Buyer's Solicitor will also be checking that any funds from their client are with him in plenty of time for completion. He is also under a duty to carry out "pre-completion" Searches. If the Buyer is having a mortgage, his Solicitor has to carry out Bankruptcy Searches against the names of each Buyer, to make sure that they have never been declared bankrupt. He will also have to carry out a Land Registry Search to check that no further entries have been made on the Seller's title since the date he received the title documents from the Seller's Solicitor at the beginning of the transaction. This Search also grants the Buyer's Solicitor a priority period in which to register the Buyer as the new owner of the property at the Land Registry.

Once all the above matters have been dealt with, everybody can relax and wait for completion!

CHAPTER 9
Completion

Moving day has arrived!

This is the day you have been waiting for, and is the day the balance purchase monies are received by the Seller's Solicitor and at which point the keys are handed over to the Buyer. When this is achieved, completion has taken place.

Unfortunately, the present system can sometimes make it difficult to predict what time of the day completion will be taking place, as all parties in the chain are reliant on receiving funds through the Banking system. The funds are sent by way of telegraphic transfer from the Buyer's Solicitor to the Seller's Solicitor. If there are only two parties in the chain, hopefully completion can take place relatively quickly as there is only one telegraphic transfer to be done. However, if there is a large chain, it can take several hours for the money to reach the top of the chain.

Predicting how long it will take for monies to be received is very difficult, because Solicitors are often reliant on their own Bank sending monies as soon as being instructed to do so, and once the transfer is in the system, it can take anything from say thirty minutes to two hours for the money to be received the other end, depending on how busy the Banking system is that day. Bearing in mind most completions happen on a Friday, it tends to mean that the Banking system is also going to be busy that day!

It is therefore a case of awaiting news from your Solicitor, once he has any, and it is very important that he has your mobile phone number to keep you informed as to progress.

The Seller's Removal Company will normally arrive at around 9.00 a.m. on completion day, and the average house removal will take approximately three to four hours. By the time the house has been emptied, hopefully the money will have been received by the Seller's Solicitor, and if so, keys can then be released. This can be done either by the Seller depositing them with his Estate Agent, or handing them over directly to the Buyer. Of course, it may be that money has been received before the Seller has had the opportunity of clearing their house, and in these circumstances, common sense normally prevails and the Buyer waits until the property is empty before moving in.

Your Solicitor will advise you in most important terms that you should never hand over the keys until you have received a telephone call from him saying that completion has taken place. Even though you may have built up a good and trusting relationship with the Buyer during the transaction, circumstances outside of the Buyer's control may mean that monies are not received by the Seller's Solicitor as they should be.

Likewise, if completion does take place on the Friday, for example, you should never agree to allow the Seller to remain in the property until the Saturday. You should always make sure that you obtain the keys and possession of the property when you are entitled to do so. Any alternative agreements agreed directly between Buyer and Seller will not normally stand up if one party does not stick to that arrangement!

Once monies have been received by the Seller's Solicitor, he will notify his client of this as well as notifying the Buyer's Solicitor and if applicable, authorises the Estate Agents to release the keys to the Buyer. He will also at this time arrange to pay off the Sellers mortgage by way of a telegraphic transfer. He will also be making arrangements to pay the Seller's Estate Agent's bill, and forwarding any balance monies to the Seller. Again, the monies due to the Seller can be paid by way of telegraphic transfer or by way of a cheque. Please note however, that most Solicitors will make a charge for sending the balance monies to the Seller by way of telegraphic transfer. Finally, he will also be sending the title documents and other relevant paperwork to the Buyer's Solicitor.

CHAPTER 10

Post-completion

Although the hard work has now been done, there is still work for both the Seller's and Buyer's Solicitor to do.

The Seller's Solicitor, who will have paid off his client's mortgage on completion, if applicable, will be awaiting a form from the Mortgage lender to confirm that the mortgage has been paid off in full. As he has provided an undertaking to the Buyer's Solicitor to do this, once the form has been received, he then sends this to the Buyer's Solicitor as evidence that he has complied with the undertaking

The Buyer's Solicitor is first under a duty to forward the Stamp Duty Land Transaction Form together with payment of any Stamp Duty to HM Revenue and Customs and this must be done within thirty days of completion. If this deadline is missed, an automatic fine is payable. Upon receipt of the form, HM Revenue and Customs will issue a certificate and this is required by the Buyer's Solicitor before the Land Registry application can be made.

Once the Stamp Duty Certificate, and where applicable, the Mortgage Discharge Form have been received, the Buyer's Solicitor can then register his client as the new owner of the property at the Land Registry. He will also be registering any mortgage on behalf of the Buyer's mortgage lender. Once the registration has been completed, the Land Registry will forward to the Buyer's Solicitor the Title Information Document. The Title Information Document is the documentary evidence showing the Buyer as the new registered owner of the property at the land Registry and is what was traditionally known as the "Title Deeds".

If you have purchased the property with the aid of a mortgage, the Title Information Document will also show this mortgage as being registered against the property, and normally the Buyer's Solicitor will be under a duty to send the Title Information Document to the mortgage lender together with the Searches and any other documentation that may be required. Banks and Building Societies have different requirements in this regard, and some do not require any documents to be sent to them following completion.

The Buyer's Solicitor will now also forward to the Buyer a copy of the Title Information Document, and depending on the mortgage lender's requirements, may also be sending you the Searches and other documents relating to the property such as planning consents and guarantees. If so, it is most important for the Buyer to keep these in a safe place, as it will be necessary to produce these documents as and when you come to sell or re-mortgage the property. However, after this lengthy process, moving house is probably the last thing on your mind!

Glossary of Legal Terms – Conveyancing

Advance	The payment of mortgage monies by the lender.
Bank Draft:	The payment of funds guaranteed by a Bank.
Bankruptcy Search:	A search carried out by the Buyer's solicitors shortly before completion to check that the Buyer is not bankrupt and has no bankruptcy petitions pending against him.
Bridging Loan:	A short-term loan.
Buildings Insurance:	A Policy to protect your property in case of damage to it.
Buyer:	The party who is purchasing the property.
Chain:	The parties involved in the specific conveyancing transaction.
Chancel Search	A search to see if a property may be called upon to contribute towards repairs to a local Church.
Charge:	A debt secured on the property. Monies borrowers from a building society or bank for the purchase of a house are usually secured against the property.

Coal Mining Search:	A search that confirms whether the property has been affected by post or current coal mining.
Commonhold:	A new type of property owners, an alternative to leasehold.
Completion:	The day on which the purchase of a property happens. The day that you move house.
Contract:	The legally binding agreement between the buyer and the seller.
Conveyancing:	General term for the legal process of buying and selling houses.
Covenants:	Rules and conditions contained in the deeds that related to the upkeep of the property.
Deposit:	Part of the purchase price (normally 10% of the purchase price) which is paid on exchange of contracts by the buyer.
Disbursements:	Out-of-pocket expenses often incurred by your solicitor.
Easements:	A right granted over another's property (such as a right of way).
Endowment Mortgage:	A mortgage covered by a policy that is designed to pay off the capital owed on the mortgage by the end of the term of the mortgage. Monthly payments are made towards the policy and towards the interest owed on the mortgage.
Environmental Search:	A report containing information on the past and current land

	use of the property and whether there is a risk of environmental contamination.
Exchange of Contracts:	The stage at which the transaction between the seller and the buyer becomes legally binding.
Freehold	Out-right ownership of the property and the land on which it stands.
Ground Rent:	Annual payments made to a landlord. This applies only to leasehold properties.
Home Information Pack:	An information pack provided by the Seller containing compulsory documents as required by legislation.
Landlord:	One who owns property and rents it to others.
Land Registry:	A Government agency that maintains records of ownership of registered land in England and Wales.
Lease:	A document made between the landlord and the tenant, setting out the terms of occupation of a property.
Leasehold:	The occupier owns the right to reside in a property for a fixed term but not the land on which is stands.
Local search:	Enquiries made of a local authority concerning planning and services.

Management Company:	A company formed to comply with a landlords' obligations.
Mortgage:	A loan secured against a property.
Mortgagee:	A money lender, such as a building society or bank, who secures the loan against the property.
Mortgage Lender:	The Bank or Building Society which grants a mortgage.
Official copy entries:	Certified copies of the title of a property obtained from the Land Registry, confirming ownership of the property.
Personal Representatives:	The person appointed by a Will to act for the deceased owner.
Redemption:	The paying off of a mortgage.
Registered Land:	Land which is registered has its ownership details recorded at the Land Registry.
Repayment Mortgage:	A mortgage where the borrower makes interest and capital payments to the lender.
Requisitions on Title:	Queries raised about the ownership of the property and how that ownership will be transferred.
Retention:	Monies held by from an Advance pending completion of building work to the property.
Service Charge:	Money requested by a landlord for repairs and maintenance to a property.
Stamp Duty Land Tax:	A tax charged to purchasers buying properties.

Subject to Contract:	Negotiations which do not become binding until contracts are exchanged.
Structural Survey:	An assessment of the essential framework of a building.
Telegraphic Transfer:	The sending of money from one Bank of another electronically.
Tenant:	A person who pays rent to another for the use of a property or land
Tenure:	The type of property: freehold of leasehold
Term:	A period of time, such as the length of a lease.
Title:	The documentary history of the ownership of the property.
Transfer:	The document which hands over the owners of the property.
Undertaking:	An assurance given by on Solicitor to another to do a specific act.
Unregistered land:	Property which is not registered at the Land Registry.
Valuation Report:	An assessment of a property's value by a lender's surveyor for the benefit of the lender.
Water/Drainage Search:	A search to check the arrangements as to drainage and water supply for a property.

Printed in Great Britain
by Amazon.co.uk, Ltd.,
Marston Gate.